AF255529

THE ARROW MAKER

Previous poetry collections by D. M. Black

With Decorum (Scorpion Press), 1967
Penguin Modern Poets 11 (with Peter Redgrove and
D. M. Thomas), 1968
The Educators (Barrie & Rockliff / Cresset Press), 1969
The Happy Crow (M. Macdonald), 1974
Gravitations (M. Macdonald), 1979
Collected Poems, 1964-1987 (Polygon), 1991
Love as Landscape Painter (translations from Goethe)
(Fras Publications), 2006
Claiming Kindred (Arc Publications, 2011)

The Arrow Maker

D. M. BLACK

ARC
PUBLICATIONS
2017

Published by Arc Publications
Nanholme Mill, Shaw Wood Road,
Todmorden OL14 6DA, UK
www.arcpublications.co.uk

978 1910345 21 4 (pbk)
978 1910345 22 1 (hbk)

ACKNOWLEDGMENTS

The author is grateful to the editors of the following magazines
in which some of these poems, or earlier versions of them, first
appeared: *Crazyhorse, Modern Poetry in Translation, Poetry London,
Poetry Review, Stand, The Dark Horse, The Long Poem Magazine,
Theology* and *Warwick Review.*

Cover image:
Detail from 'Eliezer and Rebecca at the Well'
by Nicolas Poussin
(oil on canvas, 1648)

**Editor for the UK and Ireland
John W. Clarke**

for Juliet

CONTENTS

I cannot settle my object. It goeth so unquietly and staggering, with a natural drunkenness. I take it in this plight, as it is at the instant I amuse myself about it. I describe not the essence but the passage.

Montaigne, *On Repenting*
(trs. John Florio)

Oh! Blessed rage for order, pale Ramon,
The maker's rage to order words of the sea,
Words of the fragrant portals, dimly-starred,
And of ourselves and of our origins…

Wallace Stevens
'The Idea of Order at Key West'

Not able to stay in a theme, not able to appear, this invisibility which becomes contact and obsession is due not to the nonsignifyingness of what is approached, but to a way of signifying quite different from that which connects exposition to sight.

Emmanuel Lévinas
'Otherwise than Being'
(trs. Alphonso Lingis)

I

THE ARROW-MAKER

The arrow-maker has beautiful hands: they are strong and slender.
He glues the flight to the shank with unpausing, definite movements.
With his steady gaze before him, he weighs the arrowheads in his hand –
he makes a decision, he binds one head to the shaft,
winding the tough thread round, again and again, correcting for overlaps;
then glues the thread in its place, then varnishes the length of the arrow –
then stands it to dry out of sight, in the deep shade in back of the
    door-light.

But the arrow-maker is young: he would like to be out with his mates
    catching squirrels
or gambling for beans in the village, with breaks for philosophizing
    and horse-play;
or perhaps going off with a girl, past the small fields into the forest
to which they are called by the Meaning of Life, dreaming and loving…
or he would like to be down at the river, admiring its wrestling currents
or dizzy seeing its broad, shining floor, forever in decorous motion.

It is a burden for the arrow-maker that he has to make arrows, that his
    people depend on him.
He sits in the doorway in sunlight, not looking up from his task,
or looking up when someone approaches, and calling out to them
    cheerfully.
He is identified with his task: you couldn't say he is sorrowful
or that he's proud, exactly, to have this use for his dark eyes and
    beautiful hands.

QUATRAIN

after Giordano Bruno

O my sick mind, what impedes you in giving birth to your chlldren?
 Will this stepmotherly world look with no joy at that gift?
Though dark shadows extend all over the Earth, let your summit,
 piercing through threatening night, shine in Olympian day!

SELF-RELIANCE

When a man, approaching death,
looks out over a parkland,
seeing oak-trees and roses,

and feeling, perhaps, a love
that has no natural consummation
like the love-making of man and woman

and that lives, therefore, below a skyline
of half-conscious reticence
– though the body speaks it –

he may think that when he dies
it will bring an end
to oak-trees and roses,

to colours, to freshness, to the look of the sky
that humans know –
and to a secret train of memories, in the dark cave of the heart,

that he alone knows – but, also,
though he will not be around to perceive it,
to a certain life-long artifice of self-reliance –

rather as, perhaps, when the tarred roof of an ancient shed,
green and shining with moss and lichens,
tears open, finally, and admits the weather.

AN UNEXPECTED INTIMACY

This afternoon I picked up a warm stone
– I was wanting to fix a hole that had appeared in the pathway –
and I had to check a sudden urge to apologise,
as if I had inadvertently
intruded on something to which my wants were entirely irrelevant.
I seemed to have broken in on a life that had been in progress for
     millions of years,
always uncelebrated, always in private, through heat, cold, pressure,
     exposure,
washing, melting, and grinding, and that suddenly now
on this unseasonally sunny late-October afternoon, had been plucked
     from its voiceless destiny
to become a part of the intense fast-moving transparent flood of verbally
     architected consciousness
that we call *history* in our dismayingly blinkered fashion;
and its character until that moment, which to it was to be an unthought
     piece of the breathing universe,
nameless, abiding, ceaselessly changing, without significance,
turned in my hand, and without an instant's delay, into an object of
     use and comparison,
with a purpose not its own purpose, but to do with buggies and bicycles
that it had never in all its millions of years conceived, and that it was
     certainly not equipped for understanding – and yet also, I thought,
warm like human skin, naked, and friendly, and intimate,
so that I wanted to say: *O I'm sorry! (but at the same time, how nice to
     encounter you!):*
I hadn't realised you were there.

THE PIGEON

          … This interminable wet winter,
we found a dead pigeon lying on its back
(no obvious cause of death) beside a rose-bed.
Two or three days later, overcoming some reluctance,
I prepared it for burial: two spits deep in the mounded
earth behind our Buddha who in spring
is surrounded by daffodils. I arranged the pigeon
deep in the shining clay and spaded down the overspill
over that subtle plumage; then set on top
an old heavy drain-cover to keep off the foxes,
and was turning to clean the spade when I noticed
another pigeon obsequious in the shrubbery,
hunched like a small football, and watching me.
I started toward her, as, at a funeral,
one might toward a fellow-mourner, not known but,
for an instant, kin in loss. She didn't scare, or move, and I,
aware of our difference of species, stopped halfway –
and we both stayed still then, silenced, and somehow respecting
a truth we neither of us could get on top of.

He didn't yearn to embrace every palm-tree
and gum-tree, the huge horizon, the bush,
the desert oak-trees; didn't yearn
to embrace the waterless riverbed, the red soil,
the leagues of fire-blackened bloodwood and piercing-pointed
    grasses; least of all
yearned to embrace the unassailable mastery
of the sun, that fist in the face, that wall of flame
all creatures curled from. None of these
did he yearn to embrace.
                    It was another urgency
shaped his pining, there, on the emphasized highway
straight-ruled through nameless uniquenesses. It was a wish
that was no wish, a longing, a crying-out in the cells of the body
to dissolve, to change, to be reconformed, refigured
as all that landscape, in its eternal intercourse
with itself, with the sun, the wind, the cloud,
without the impedimenta of words and language
and the fretting for a point of view, for the characterful voice
that speaks and makes the speaking universe tongue-tied.
It was another sort of thing from a wish;
it was not a wish.

I saw him through a window of the tube-train,
a swarthy man, not youthful, dressed in tired,
all-weather clothing. He was out on the platform
and I inside, observing. As the doors
opened, he swung two heavy suitcases,
battered, unlabelled, up and through the doorway,
then turned to the remaining, cardboard box. And as he did,
the doors started to close; he rushed to hold them
and missed his grip, and failed, and the doors shut,
and he outside, a ghost. Someone said:
Push the button! As if some button would
reverse the train, but there was no button
or not one one could find, and now already
we were in the tunnel. A tall woman
said: *One's worst nightmare.* The blockish cases stood
on end, grazed, grainy, poverty-stricken,
telling us nothing. The woman spoke
with her companion: they would take the cases
out of the train at the next station; she
would stand beside them, he would go to find
the station controller: thus, they thought, the man
would have his best chance to retrieve his luggage.
It wasn't clear what we'd all witnessed but
they meant to solve it: for all they knew,
it might have been unreined catastrophe.

YAMANE-SAN

She told me that before the Emperor made his announcement
she walked around the streets of the quarter
and said goodbye to them, one after the other.
She was eight years old,
she did not wish to die,
but she knew it was their destiny, theirs and hers.

When finally the Emperor spoke on the radio
he spoke with such noble diffidence
that nobody was perfectly certain they had understood him.
This was so especially
because what he said was a contradiction
of what they all knew to be destiny.

The following evening
she again walked out around the quarter.
She saluted the surviving streets.
She congratulated them on their survival.
They seemed rather sombre.
She was not sure that she was pleased to see them,
nor was she quite sure that they were pleased
with their altered destiny.

The fate of war defines the population.
So many were living whom we thought the future.
Now, these remain here. Not the best,
or bravest, or most beautiful, or the ones
we loved most fiercely, but the ones that have
endured, in holes and corners, from behind
tree-trunks, old barns, from under-the-floorboards, these,
like Aphrodite on a flood of tears,
are borne toward us, begging that we forgive them,
that we endorse them. Dead friends, dead lovers,
how can we talk to them and not betray you?
Are we wrong to think you beg us to betray you?

"UNTARRYINGLY-COMING"

This elated adjective – he then deleted it – the poet
Paul Celan
thought of writing in the Visitors' Book
of the philosopher Martin Heidegger.

What did Celan's adjective describe?
It described the true
word that might rise in the profound heart
of the great philosopher,

a word, lovely as water, that the ex-Nazi
might speak to the Jew
and both behold
an unbelievable rainbow!

Alas, Heidegger
had no word
(though he had words like rainbows,
in abundance, ravishing…).

When the time came to plan his next visit,
Paul Celan
drowned himself in the Seine
and tarried in Paris.

GLOBAL CLIMATE CHANGE

The raven himself is hoarse...
Macbeth

Those tonnes of metal at the speed of rifle-bullets
crack down the motorway. In each of them
a sovereign citizen with his wits about him
does what the others do: he knows he's safe.
While you alone, unnerved on the hard shoulder,
facing cold steel, and stunned, are shot to pieces...

You learn at first hand the plight of the mentally ill:
to be broken down, marginalized, and appalled by health.

Those who refused to look through the telescope
of seductive Galileo were perhaps far-sighted:
I think they foresaw the rise of the lightning conductor,
the improvements in surgical hygiene, the increase in the
    production of pig-iron,
the scooting-off-down-the-track of the first steam-engine, the
    formulation of Coca-cola,
the launch of Sputnik, the worldwide sale of the dish-washer,
the ascent of the share-price of Apple, the arrival of universal
    surveillance,
the poisoning of all the world's oceans, nuclear weapons in the
    hands of madmen,
the choking of the earth's atmosphere, the dying of all the world's
    animals…
and they said: 'You know what, Galileo Galilei? –
we are far-sighted; we have telescopes of our own; we
have seen the moons of Jupiter. Thank you! Good-bye!'

WARD LECTURE

"They're strange, these neurological conditions.
Here is a strong man, crashed upon his back
beside his bed. The nurses rush around,
hoist him back up, repair his wounds and gashes,
then leave him to himself. He swings his body
at once out of the sheets, sets foot to floor,
and stands, and crashes, helpless as before,
and brings the nurses running, all aflutter,
to lift him up again, and mend his bruises.

While you, meanwhile,
the startled onlooker, can see exactly
how this is happening. One leg is amputated
and so he crashes, making no attempt
to balance, or support himself with a crutch.
But then – why not? It's that his mind's unable
to learn his leg has vanished; it refuses
to suffer an irreparable loss."

1

He needed women in a different way
in those days. Where women were
was where fear was not; and though he loved
the frightening world, to find the bragging voice,
the belly-laugh proclaiming he had courage,
he had to go back to the cooking-pots and clutter.
Not that they were not frightening too,
those raucous mothers, shapeless like the ocean,
now full, now empty; now hot with sex and now
so heart-breakingly mortal few had strength enough
to become the string-thighed, wizened-breasted ancients
who clawed him like the wait-a-bit thorn and would not
quit his mind however hard he abandoned them.
They became him; he couldn't shake them off.

2

                    'In those days' too,
the lithe, insatiable girls were last year's children.
Forthright, enchanting, on a summer evening
one led him out like music into the forest, and
was his! Like timid Adam after Eve's creation,
he woke next morning in a flawless world:
both body and soul for once had found relief,
and liked each other!
He was possessed; but how could she now be this
Pandora's bag of crude and stinging voices?
He hated what he saw: her slammed against
the walls of her provocative, snake-like body,
and swelling, a melon swallowing-up the flower;
then joined with the women, become his jeering critic.

– He didn't understand and didn't wish to!
He loved to hunt with the men: on the forest floor
his stealing steps entranced him; the pre-dawn mystery,
the horned, wise antelopes, the fear all round him…
Son of Man! you knew yourself in those sweet singing
moments, and you hymned the world incessantly.

3

Now on a different floor he stands at ease
by the sink in a sunlit kitchen, coming events
casting their radiance before. His daughter
brightens the sunlight as she talks, her smiling
eyes on his, and he is smiling too,
though serious. He jokes – what will they call
the as-yet-ungendered infant? – and their agenda
is practical: prenatal yoga, breast-feeding,
and the years that are taken for granted. He
is calm, delighted, and restrains
as best he can the astonishment within. How
from the womb of time is born this absolute newness,
never predicted, never to be repeated!
Outside the window, goldfinches quarrel in the tamarisk.
Sweet sunlight sparks along the chrome of the taps.

1. Classical

> *"Tard, très tard, je t'ai connue, la Tristesse"*
> – Ezra Pound

                         Perhaps you wondered, Ezra,
since you thought so much about wisdom,
by what marks we recognize it; how, for example,
to know if wisdom's recommendation
was to remain Hugh Selwyn Mauberley and not offer,
maddened by his radiance, to compete with Apollo?
Wasn't there some German poet I half-remember
who walked the width of France, eyes fried by the sun,
and declared himself on arrival blessed, not crazy?
That was Apollo's horse-play. Patron of mice,
crusher of pythons, healer, guitarist, body-
builder and merciless bowman – a god for groupies:
and here they are, all Nine of them, on Parnassus.
It takes keen eyes
to track this murderous god, not, like yours, blinded
by tears shed over a "botched civilization"
or, better said, by the squinting brilliance
of tears shut down on. We know
that those who will not be sad become angry,
and those who will not put the gods in their place
go mad with adoration. Flayed by beauty,
torn between women and high on half-read heroes,
you met some Bottom-with-the-head-of-a-donkey
and fell for him! You with an ear and eye
as sharp as any in poetry, fell for that pumped-up
fraudster's bombast and forgot
that courage lay in mastering vanity
and not in swooning when some manly jawbone
beckoned you to the latrines…
                         We who loved you still

continued to watch you, like a swimmer, lifting
alternate arms and shoulders into the sunlight
("when the raft broke and the waters went over me"
and no white seagull came to alight on the flotsam
in that lost cold and loveless Ocean). You
never stopped talking, till the sadness crashed
finally over you in a sort of torpor, where
you sat, eyes dazzled,
greatness an *ignis fatuus* fluttering near you –
Bottom now plainly Bottom, Apollo –
where was Apollo who had seemed to parent
that silken, luminous dawn, your "radiant world"?

2. Christian

> "Painting the Crucifixion made me ill, I took such pains with it.
> Do not insist, I beg you."
> > – Nicolas Poussin

If Shostakovich in his Second Piano Trio
envisaged "the horrible forced dance of Jews
before they were machine-gunned to death", that
would not have seemed outlandish to Jesus
at this moment. He stands in the Jordan river,
having water poured over his head by a man in animal-skins,
and seeing, in the air, a dove descending
and hearing, vast above him, a paternal voice
crack the blue sky with its gigantic detonation:
"THIS IS MY SON!
THIS IS MY BELOVED SON, IN WHOM
I AM WELL PLEASED!!"
– And now there will be no
kindly deviation
from what's before him, stabler than the landscape:

black fear-filled night in the ancient olive orchard,
sweat like blood, the sudden shouts, the torchlight,
the pitiless flogging, the shoulder-shrugging officials,
the off-hand condemnation –
the cross's tenth-rate wood, the faceted nails
(he knows about carpentry) – the sickening swing
that takes him up to the vertical –
the caress of the murdering, unbearable sun –
until that final cry of one discarded,
dying incredulous this was what he'd amounted to –

He goes with heavy steps and plods off into
the iron desert. Meek is not the word
and nor is angry either: he accepts God's fiat,
knowing all this is necessary, is the fate
of mortal man who does not choose his epoch:
like many in my lifetime, Jews, Russians, Germans,
Afghans, Iraqis, uncomprehending
poor gale-flung debris forced to march or shuffle
through a war-lit landscape stunned by war's machinery.

Iphigeneia – dear girl –
slight, but your head high –
you walk with a coltish stumble
as you approach the fire and the altar.

You know, and the whole army knows,
that the Goddess withholds
the wind stretching towards Helen
from Agamemnon.

A stern appetite
– *sacrifice!* –
possesses the ranks of warriors.
You are like unprepared food.

You are unfrightened by the glittering blade.
You inhale proudly.
– *Iphigeneia! those are your Daddy's ships,*
black on the Ocean!

'C'EST TROP FACILE': REMEMBERING JACQUES BREL ON THE M6

Comme un ivrogne je partirai
pour aller gueuler ma chanson...
                    – Jacques Brel

Blinded by squalling rain, approaching Shap,
I slap the headlights on and slow to sixty,
and in that dizzying opal twilight, against
the hammering windscreen wipers, comes your voice,
grand Jacques, which is the voice of everyman –
or the voice of everyman could he but unchain it.
You say it is too easy
to make pretence, and maybe you never waited
for Madeleine with lilacs, or commanded the maid
to change the sheets because Matilda was back –
Maudite Matilde! puisque te v'là!! –
or when Madame
paraded her ass on the ramparts of Warsaw
perhaps you were not in reality
washing the dishes back at the Alcazar.
Nevertheless you were, like all of us, always
the heroic loser in those bitter romances,
and only your transcendent voice proclaimed
some freedom in such failure. Even the sailors
in Amsterdam, munching their cod and chips,
who pissed while you sobbed over unfaithful women,
seemed, unlike you, to manage the world, enclosed
in masculinity, in that pretence
your truthfulness forbade you. Yours became the voice
of all men suffering virility
and too much love of beauty, too much compassion
for the old, the lost, for those dying
unjustly like Jaurès. When with lovely
nakedness you sang: *belle jeunesse!*, we heard
the love and pain of one condemned like us
to bear a human life, and be fobbed off

with whisky and cinemas. And with beer
from London to Berlin…!
                                    Like a drunk
you went your ways, to give that unchained throat
to serve those heartfelt songs, of which, you said,
you were the shadow.
                            But *tais-toi donc, grand Jacques,*
que connais-tu de tout ça? The night you died
a Québecoise of my acquaintance took me out
forcefully on a pub-crawl through the squares of London
to speak the grief she felt, and shared with tens of
thousands of others. It may be easy
to make pretence, but she – and I too – knew
she had met you intimately, knowing what you made
with your unappeasable voice.
                                    – I wake from reverie:
white clouds and sunlight over Scotland's border!
and find the headlights on. I switch them off.

IN ST. PETER'S, ROME

Through layers
of crystalline rock the heart's exploding hammer
clatters, goes deeper, cries out for the lack
of true companionship. If twice or thrice
in a long lifetime you found that lack fulfilled,
you hold those memories. Once more in St. Peter's Basilica,
approaching Michelangelo's Pietà,
you sense the loveliness and the not-quite-right
of this religion: the adult son, come home
to his youthful mother, and she has him now
for all eternity. – That's not it, exactly,
though the weeping marble truly bodies something
of the heart's clamour. It's no use
to seek in frames, in polished limestone, what
is asked of a living world, of rock and sunlight,
of cloud and cities. But now a subtler shadow,
from years ago, insists, against this bronze
airy and porphyry'd vastness, on recalling
me to a basement, somewhere off Notting Hill,
tea and sweet biscuits on a plastic table-cloth,
and I am saying something – I forget –
exuberant, and exaggerated, and
the American Hindu monk, Swami Yogeshananda,
laughs, calls across to me: *David, remember:*
truth is the austerity of the Kali-Yuga!
and discovering him, my mendacious heart is quieted.

– As it has been before: it's the contour
that counts, the profile-during-time
that can't be stilled but must, if it's
to be caught be clung to, like the Old Man of the Sea
– now fire, now repulsive snake, now human body –
who if embraced with reckless perseverance
may speak eventually with a sort of wisdom.

II

SAINT AUGUSTINE'S EULOGY FOR HIS MOTHER, SAINT MONICA

                              … Not only I – she
too once drank from the wine-barrel, in florid rebellion
against her esteemable mother. But the Lord
in the shape of a serving girl, told her parents, who
led her back to the way of righteousness. Later, a
wife among wives, she
taught them the holy duty of acquiescence
in the will of a husband who is woman's master, even when he
beats her unjustly. Not a lesson Eve's self-loving daughters were
eager to learn! You know, Lord God,
how the soul is born out of such earthly diminishments
and finds its nourishment in a spiritual country
unlike the world of those who pine in palaces
or preen in the provocations of fashion. I too, sinner and
son of that violent husband, drank from that barrel
and then (for fourteen years! bowed low by the body's
deforming appetites) from that woman you sent me
to shame me more thoroughly and, by losing her, to
break my heart to bleeding and to thereby
make my soul; with whom too
I made this son – 'God's gift', we called him, blasphemously,
and yet, perhaps, not entirely mistakenly –
who stands there now, a tall, intelligent youth,
not like these Ostian peasants, and resembling his mother
whose image haunts me still, in him and in my
nightly dreams. How can your mercy pardon
such carnal obstinacy! such a wall of sin! So sunk in wickedness my
heart I told my mother a lie and so escaped her
to Rome and thence to Milan, lusting for trifles
of rank and title, human commendations
of no meaning in your sight. There she found me,
my never-resting parent; there she weaned me

from that vile barrel, that travesty of your breast
and your sweet milk of truth. I put away
my concubine and suffered *dolor pectoris*,
pain in the chest beholding that vacuity
in which my soul had sported, dead to the
promise of true joy – and dead to *her*,
whose only care was my eternal welfare.

     – And now she's died,
my tireless mother, having led me to you,
having served you loyally till the *nunc dimittis*;
and for such toil now rightly gains her freedom,
and hears her Master calling: *Come, you faithful
servant, come and be seated at your Master's table,
and wear the crown reserved for the unswerving.*

THE SIZE OF THINGS

(A reflection on the doctrine of the Trinity)

What a huge statement for such little people!
each one a fathom long, or in the Middle Ages
less than a fathom, as I am myself. And yet
each dared to trust to something, and to imagine
in passionate colloquy across the centuries
what *God is love*, that facile, stark equation
means when you spell it out. Not just the universe,
the stars and galaxies, greater itself
than the reach of human thought, but they went further
to conceive the inconceivable Vis-à-vis,
actor-director on this sun-charred, moon-
haunted, storm-lit, earthquake-jolted stage,
this props-and-scenery for moral action
as to them it came, increasingly, to seem –

Without laboratories, without research grants,
alone and furious, desperate with worship,
they interrogated the void and found this cradle,
this structured emptiness, this Three-in-One,
that defeated logic but in perichoresis
turned in a dance of love, twirling the stars
like gearwheels, like the hands of Highland dancers
who whirl their lovers, and pull in even the wallflowers –

even the maidenly, intellectual atheists.
They knew the size of things was never the point.

There is no mystery of Incarnation:
the body is the impersoning of the divine
and does not cease to be body. This George Fox learned
when he took off his shoes and socks and walked through Lichfield,
and saw in the market-place a lake of blood
and channels of blood pouring down every alley.
He adopted prophetic mode and shouted *Woe!*
Woe to the bloody city of Lichfield!
until his friends came up to him and said *Alack,*
George, where are thy shoes? being concerned,
as friends are, more for the present body
than for that tremendous vision, which he discovered later
was of the blood of martyrs from the time of Diocletian
fourteen centuries previously –

for one has to find some story to explain
the measureless rage in a loving, dignified man,
so lit by the Lord's blaze that he left it to others
to notice – what of course they noticed at once – the stark
mud, and the stones cutting his feet.

Once, robed and through a frozen dawn, Saint Francis
went begging bread. His feet were blue to see.
But his heart, not governed by his circumstances,
blazed like a bonfire in his dauntless bosom.
'O, tell me of God!' he cried to a leafless tree.
The tree was an almond: it burst into blossom.

Without joy there can be no salvation
and without love there can be no joy.
I have therefore arranged with the authorities
(who were powerless, after all, to refuse me)
that whoever greets my love
with a rush of unbounded gratitude
shall be reborn in the realm of joy.
After that, the journey is a single step,
but you will be in no hurry to take it,
for to perceive love is to become able to love,
and to love is to learn to wait
with infinite kindness.

Everyone thought he was wonderful but he despised them. He knew he was not yet wonderful enough. He knew there had been others down the ages, who had founded religions, philosophies, schools of literature – they were the wonderful ones and he had not yet made it. – Or had he, perhaps? He glared at his admirers, and thought they were silly: they could never create a convincing School, even if he had achieved greatness, and of course he hadn't, how could they be so foolish as to speak like that? He sat behind his eyes, in glum rage. But he loved the true greats, those historical figures. He never doubted them. He had heard of them in school. When he spoke their names, he inhaled involuntarily, and his eyes flashed. What would *they* have thought of his admirers? Nothing!

This other one was hurt by everything. In pain he swam like a salmon, and he had names for all pain's reefs and shoals and sandbanks. He sat behind his eyes but you sensed him always coming towards you, you were never alone with his loving, eager accompaniment. He knew you well, he knew the baby, the child, the adolescent you had been and he spoke with them freely despite your presence. You were your many selves and he was the multi-reflecting jewel of Buddhism, the seer of all, that is itself a vacancy. Did he have admirers? He did indeed, he had many admirers, each one himself or herself, who went away with a sense of gratitude and also a sort of astonishment, to have been known so suddenly and so intimately and yet to have encountered no one.

After they both died there was a sense that giants had walked on the earth. But it was hard to be sure. As time went on, they became more gigantic.

"To be or not to be, is that the question, Hamlet? Is that the first and final question? Is human *being* a matter of compelling oneself to *be*, and does the understanding of *being*, the dextrous wielding of the verb *to be*, constitute the first philosophy required by a consciousness that from the outset is made up of knowledge and representations of the world; that from the outset defines itself by its opposition to death, as a lucidity of continuing thought, thrusting forward even into death itself; that must in its precarious finitude find itself forever either on the one hand heroic or, on the other, anguished?

"Or is the first question rather that of the uncomfortable conscience, that uneasy awareness that is by no means the same as the consciousness to which death is the threat, death is the enemy? Such unease of conscience questions my *right to be*, questions my right to the power to affect an Other, including even, at the ultimate extreme, my right to cause *his* death, to extinguish *his being*. In the light of these questions, my innocent wish to *carry on being* appears a mere amiable naivety. The right *to be*, and the legitimacy of that right, are not derived finally from some abstract and universal Law, but they have to stand unashamed in the face of an Other to whom I am unable to be indifferent. Regardless of how he regards me, for me, when I perceive his face, indifference has become impossible.

"With this question, life awakens to the dimension of the human. Prince! *écoute-moi*. The question is not about *to be*, that extraordinary verb, but about its justification. We arrive here at the supreme question: not, why is there *being* rather than nothingness? but, *what am I* in the light of this claim on my concern of an Other to whom I cannot be indifferent? In what universe do I discover myself to awaken?"

WILLIAM YEATS'S LAMENT FOR LADY AUGUSTA GREGORY

I put my feelings in a verse
and this is what I said:
'What shall I do for pretty girls
now my old bawd is dead?'

I did not say it for a joke
or to create effect,
though some who heard it looked away
and said I lacked respect,

but those who knew the Muses well
knew what my Muse had said:
the pretty girls were pretty still,
but my old bawd was dead.

DECODING THE ORACLE

I'd not cared to hear the Sibyl rave,
I did not trek to the Sibyl's cave,
but regardless of that she turned up at my place
and showed me three masks for the ageing face.

One looked back with bitter tears;
one looked ahead with shuddering fears;
and one looked out on the present day
with rage at all folk do and say.

I praised the Sibyl and wished her well,
but I didn't buy what she'd brought to sell;
I thought what she brought to me foretold
true sharks in the water of growing old.

She spoke not a word when I said goodbye,
but I read her thought by the glint in her eye –
and I knew that she knew that we humankind
need a human face to meet our mind.

MINIATURES

A RUBAI FOR A FOREFATHER

When that Devonian Fish, my Ancestor
(and yours), climbed up onto some Granite Shore,
and, first in all of Time, beheld the Moon –
did he not stand, and give a Lion's Roar?

THE RAILROAD TRACK

I love, by the rusting
railroad track,
willowherb and buddleia
growing back,

telling how beauty
will go on
when raucous mankind has roared
past and gone.

MY WRETCHED SPECIES

My wretched species believes it must take over the planet,
down to its quarks and gluons; and it will do so.
Be grateful then that you lived at a time of hawthorn blossoms,
when the puffins whirred up from the water, the thrift in drifts…

AN ELDERLY JEW IN RICHMOND PARK

Phantoms concern him. Here and now
is not for him the present scene.
The laws of heaven and earth allow
those weeping ghosts to still be seen.

A. E. H.

> *And so to church went she,*
> *And would not wait for me.*
>   – A. E. HOUSMAN: 'Bredon Hill'

He wasn't doing clever things with pronouns
when he, though gay, wrote *she* to mean his love;
but all the later *he's* that he abandoned
were *I's* to see what "I" could not believe.

EVENT IN SUMMER

I shall die and not have understood
what happened when a pigeon
alit on the branch of a chestnut-tree,
and the branch swayed and recovered –

Those who slaughter sacrificial
lambs for Passover must learn to
do so neatly with no broken
bones; therefore, on that Friday
when the executed felons
had to be deposed by nightfall,
soldiers broke their legs to speed the
process on; but did not break the
knees of Jesus, thus fulfilling
what the prophet had foreseen: "there
shall no bone of his be broken".
Subtle Frank Kermode debating
what is fact and what figura
held that by interpretation
we can wrestle with the angel,
Meaning, and no bone be broken.
My bones are not made so break-proof!
They will break, like rocks and mountains
and figura's formulations,
and will drift through clouds and oceans
into inter-stellar space. If
what is sought is what would let one
find one single life sufficient,
and permit a grounded joy to
undergird one's fickle surface,
it is not some deep figura
or some shrewd interpretation
that is called for, but the present
world refigured in its substance.

III

O lady, weep no more, lest I give cause
To be suspected of more tenderness
Than doth become a man.

– CYMBELINE

DER KÜRENBERGER: 'The Falcon'

I raised me a falcon   longer than a year.
When I had trained him   to my pleasure
and on his feathers   hung fine gold,
he rose up and flew   to other lands.

Later I saw the falcon   flying beautifully:
he bore on his feet   silken ribbons
and all his feathers were   golden red.
May God bring together   all who love!

BIRTHDAY POEM FOR AN ASYLUM-SEEKER

Dites-nous donc, la belle,
où donc est vot' mari?

— A. Joubert: 'Auprès de ma blonde'

In that
foreign land
in that
foreign land
in that
war

no one was with my mother – others
must have been present –
to praise her for doing well
to tell her that she had born the Messiah
that for all that blood and pain
she remained beautiful

if you were staging a competition
for the darkest hour of the planet's history
(so far, at any rate)
November, 1941
would be a fair candidate

Il est dans la Hollande...

she never named
the terror into which she peered
but a tune took me captive
by which I am still enraptured

what would you give, la belle
to be a joyful wife?
what would you give, la belle
to have your husband safe?

I would give all I own
O and my heart
my heart that thoughtless bird
that weeps both day and night

And to you, Rebecca, this old man was an angel.
You know them, not by themselves alone, but also by the
    circumstances,
and on this occasion you were not in a hurry, not caught up in
    conversation,
so when he said to you, quite unexpectedly, *Would you give
    me a drink of water?*
it seemed natural to reply, *Of course, old man, and let me water
    your camels also.*
– When the time is right, the key turns in the lock.
When the time is right, the clouds are rimmed with choirs
    of angels.
You knew at once that all was well, that something transparent
    and irrevocable had happened,
that earth was now on a new orbit
and set in a deeper channel. I think, as you poured the water,
that you had become all women, all who say Yes and refuse to fear,
or all who, in the service of love, forget their fear,
and if they think of crucifixions, they overlook them.

Love and the gentle heart are one thing only.
This the wise poet told us in his poem:
no more can one appear without the other
than the rational soul appear with reason absent.

When nature is amorous, then she creates them:
Love as the Master and the heart his mansion,
in which, lying asleep, Love takes his rest,
sometimes for a short while and sometimes for longer.

It's then that Beauty appears in a wise woman,
so pleasing to the eyes that in the heart
desire is born towards this pleasing object;

and Beauty lingers there for long enough
to waken from his sleep the spirit of Love.
It's the same for a woman with a virtuous man.

1

Adorable waif
cropped hair, huge eyes and all-too-ready grin
du kennst das Land

and I would like to wrap you in a vine-leaf
and protect you from everyone

2

On the back of the tee-shirt of the young spiritual healer
whose father was a spiritual healer
and whose grandfather was a medium
I catch myself reading
Can I pull your
Tennents Pilsner

3

O genou de Marie-Claude
O genou de Geneviève
from what ecstasies of carnal imagining
do the drifting fabrics of meditation veil us

4

The very slight very blonde young woman
with the very blue eyes
calls me over to smell the roses
and tells me she has twice had cancer

5

High in the dawn clouds
the moon is shrunk to its last diminuendo.
'There might have been no moon.'
That is unthinkable.
Nothing to pine and revive and to lead the heart
as it leads the oceans.
'There might have been no sun.'
Equally inconceivable.
We are utterly held in the web of the universe
'like a net of reflecting jewels'

6

This French girl, eyes out of Renoir,
wearing soft colours,
lives in continual dialogue.
Her gaze fixes that of her interlocutor,
her face is kindly and open and always attentive,
her body sways and holds still in the rhythm of the exchange.
And I think when I meet her
I have been blessed with a vision
of the Bodhisattva of Infinite Conversation

7

There are many truths:
'All sentient beings are the same
all seek after happiness
all strive to avoid suffering' –
yet to me what an infinite distance

between my friend witty as Kierkegaard
(she wears the same spectacles)
and this fat woman with the air of discontent
who pushes past me disagreeably in the breakfast queue

8

Parfois, à la fin de la journée,
Monsieur le Général
walks quietly among his relaxing troops.
He nods and smiles, speaks little,
but his battledress and his solidity of purpose
create a gravity
that causes the soldier with the drying-up cloth to exclaim:
'Hey! did you see him? That was the General.'

9

When the young she-wolf trots up to the male
with an air of enquiry
one ear cocked, her brow focused
her whole face smiling and challenging
she is not more beautiful
than this young Dutch woman
who is three days fallen in love

THOSE WHO WERE MORE REMARKABLE

Why is it you I forget
when I think of trees,
sensible ash-tree?
You were the good-looking house-prefect
with the well-cut hair
and the smart blazer,
whose skirt was never embarrassingly short
and who never said anything foolish.
You were not that miraculous, beautiful one, the beech-tree,
nor oak, that rock of character
– the one who always took charge,
and who turned out to be manic depressive –
nor slight birch, the all-too-vulnerable, whom I yearned to make
    part of the family,
nor poplar, ever-spontaneous, on whom no one would dream
    of relying.
You were not that great city, the lime-tree, abuzz with her
    million conversations,
nor chestnut-tree, middle-aged from girlhood,
nor Scots pine, tall and mysterious, the rangy one,
nor monkey-puzzle, the fat one, forever snagged on something
    vexatious.
How come I overlooked you, ash-tree,
how did I always overlook you,
always intrigued by those who were more remarkable?

The plant uses the energy of sunlight
to prise apart the water-molecules
and sends free oxygen out into the *Umwelt*;
meanwhile the electron and the hydrogen ion
combine with CO_2 to build the complex
hydrocarbons of branch and twig and leaf
and bud and petal. And can this explain
the joy of summer? Lovers on the lawns,
breathing pure oxygen and drunk with colours,
need not enquire too nicely of their neurons
what makes them think the Earth requires response;
and yet their question, *Is this truly love,*
or just the season? delineates a world
beyond the reach of rose or chestnut blossom.

The flesh is packed with wishes
as the sea is filled with fishes,
for when you fall into the sea
you always disturb two, or three;
and they welcome this disturbance,
they say, 'are you coming to live among us?'
for fishes are friendly creatures
and they react according to their natures.
Feckless Man, Eve's son,
would like with every one
to make his home:
John Dory, coral comb,
flounders with roaming eye,
sea-horses, octopi,
mermaids, marlins, bluefish, dabs,
prancing lobsters, stately crabs,
coelacanths from Africa
and the wicked remora,
fish with stripes, or lamps, or tresses,
fish in long transparent dresses,
drowned men, whose eyes are pearls,
dugongs, dolphins, diving girls,
sharks and rays, electric eels,
sage walruses and dog-like seals,
glum blobfish, who say 'alas!',
idle jellyfish, and wrasse,
and the many sorts of bass
– of each the sinner's heart
would choose to take their part,
not knowing, or not caring
drowning comes of such sharing.
Therefore when you go among fishes,
resemble the well-instructed Ulysses,
who visiting Sirens
had himself secured in irons.

IV

*Dante has passed through the Inferno and is now ascending the
mountain of Purgatory; Virgil continues to be his guide. At the start
of the Canto, Dante is emerging from the third Terrace, that of the
Wrathful, where the fog is so thick that he has been unable to see.
In the course of the Canto, he and Virgil climb to the fourth Terrace,
that of the Slothful.*

Recollect, reader, if ever in the mountains
you were caught in cloud so dense you could not see
except by looking through your skin, like a mole,

how, when at last those wet and sluggish vapours
began to dissipate, the sphere of the sun
seemed to insert itself weakly among them;

and then your imagination readily
will picture how it was when I could first
re-see the sun, by now already setting.

So, matching my own steps to the steady pace
of Virgil, I came out from such a cloud
to rays already dead along the shoreline.

O Imagination! which at times so robs us
from the outer world that we pay no attention
even though a thousand trumpets blast around us,

who moves you, when sensation gives you nothing?
A light moves you, that takes form in the heavens
by itself, or by a will that guides it downward.

The wickedness of her who changed her shape
to that of the bird that sings with most delight
now showed a trace in my imagination;

and with this thought my mind so far retreated
into itself that nothing from the outside
could penetrate within and be received there.

Then from the Phantasy above rained down
one, crucified, contemptuous and fierce
by his appearance, and he was dying thus;

around him were the great Ahasuerus,
his wife Esther, and the just Mordecai
who had such probity both in word and deed.

And as this imagery all broke up
of itself, like bubbles when they lack the water
they need if they are to retain their shape,

a weeping girl arose within my vision,
a child, in bitter grief, who said: 'O Queen,
why did you in your rage choose to be nothing?

You killed yourself to not lose your Lavinia
– now you have lost me! I am she that mourns,
Mother, now for your ruin more than for the other!'

As sleep is broken suddenly by new light
that strikes on the closed gaze – and then, though broken,
still quivers slightly before it dies entirely –

so these imaginings fell away as soon
as light reached me, and struck my face, far brighter
than any light to which we are accustomed.

I was turning, confused, to make out where I was
when a voice said to me: 'Here is the ascent',
and drove all other thoughts out of my mind.

That voice inspired in me a wish so urgent
to see who it was who had thus spoken to me
that it'll not rest until it sees his face.

But as the sun that weighs down on our sight
conceals its own shape by its sovereignty,
so in this matter too my power failed me.

'This is a holy spirit, who directs us,
without our asking, to the upward path,
and always by his light keeps himself hidden.

He does with us as men do with themselves:
for he who sees a need but waits for asking
is cynically preparing to reject it.

Now let our bodies move to match his summons;
let's try to make the ascent before it darkens,
for nothing's possible then, till day returns.'

Thus my guide said to me, and I and he
together turned our steps to climb the stairway,
and as soon as I set foot on the first stair

I felt a movement nearby like a wing
brushing my face, and heard: *'Blessed are they
who make peace,* who are free from wicked anger.'

Already above us now so high were lifted
daylight's last rays, which night succeeds, that on
all sides the stars were starting to appear.

'O my energy, what's causing you to falter?'
I said within myself, for I was sensing
the power in my legs come to a ceasefire.

We had reached to where the stairway climbed no higher
and there come to a standstill, like a boat
that's suddenly been run up on the beach.

I paused there for a moment, listening
for anything that told of this new Circle,
then turned back to my master, asking him:

'My gentle father, tell me, in this Circle
what is the offence that souls come here to purge?
Let your speech flow, unlike our halted footsteps.'

My master answered: 'Insufficient love
for what is good can at this stage be mended;
here the too-idle oar is plied afresh.

But to enlarge your understanding further,
consider what I say, and you will pluck
a useful fruit from this enforced delay.

Neither the Creator nor the creature ever,
my son,' he started, 'can be void of love
either from nature or the heart: you know this.

The natural is always without error,
but the heart can err by choosing a wrong object
or by excessive or too little ardour.

If the heart is focussed on the primal good
and keeps the secondary in proportion,
it cannot be the cause of evil pleasure;

but if it twists to evil, or pursues
the good with less or more care than is fitting,
the created works against its own Creator.

From this you may understand that of necessity
Love is the seed in you of every virtue
and every act that calls for condemnation.

Now since Love cannot ever turn his face
against the welfare of the one who loves,
all subjects are secure against self-hatred;

and since it is not possible to conceive
a being sundered from the Source, and standing
alone, hatred of God too is precluded.

It follows, if I judge these matters rightly,
that evil when it's loved must be another's;
such love is born three ways within your clay.

There is he who thinks he is excellent by competing
against his neighbour, and for that sole reason
he craves the downfall of his neighbour's greatness;

there's he who fears fame, love, power, honour, all
will be lost if his neighbour rises past him
and is so bitter therefore that he loves the opposite;

and he for whom insult is so injurious
that he becomes a glutton for revenge
and must then stamp his evil on the other.

This three-formed love is wept for in the three
Circles below us. Now turn your mind to think of
love that pursues good but is disproportioned.

Here each confusedly conceives a good
that will, he thinks, appease his heart's desire,
and therefore strives to unite himself with it;

but if half-hearted love draws you to knowing
it, or attaining it, then in this Circle,
having rightly grieved for that weak love, you suffer.

This other good too does not make men blissful:
it is not bliss, nor is it the essential Goodness
that is both fruit and root of all true good.

Love that abandons itself too much to this
is wept above us in the next three Circles;
but why we should conceive it as tripartite

my silence leaves you to research yourself.'

Dante has reached the lowest level of Paradise, the circle of the Moon. His guide is now Beatrice, who took over from Virgil at the top of Purgatory. In the previous Canto he has met Piccarda Donati, a woman whom he knew in Florence. She told him her story: she had joined the Poor Clares (the female branch of the Franciscans), taken vows of chastity, but then been forced out of the convent by her violent brother Corso, who compelled her to break her vows and make a marriage politically advantageous to himself. She died soon after. At the start of the present Canto, she has faded from view, along with another woman, Costanza, who had a similar history and of whom Piccarda spoke admiringly. Dante is left moved by Piccarda's story, but also troubled by certain questions he can't quite bring himself to formulate.

Between two foods, equally near, equally
enticing, the free man would starve to death
before he set his teeth in either of them;

just so a lamb might stand in parallel terror
between the slaverings of two dangerous wolves,
or a hunting-dog might stand between two deer:

and so, if I kept silent, torn between
two equal doubts, I do not blame myself,
for it was of necessity – nor commend.

Though I was silent, my desire was painted,
and with it my perplexity, more warmly
across my face than if I'd spoken clearly.

Beatrice then did as Daniel did when he
released King Nebuchadnezzar from the anger
that had made the King become unjustly cruel.

She said: 'I clearly see how you are tugged by
first one wish then the other, so your ardour
has got entangled and can't find its breath.

You argue thus: "if my right will persists,
by what good reason can another's violence
reduce the credit due to my deserving?"

Also, it causes you to doubt because
it seems that souls might go back to the stars
as Plato taught, but not as Christians think.

These are the questions that weigh equally
upon your will; however, I will first
address the one that is more poisonous.

Not the great Seraph who's most one with God,
nor Moses, Samuel, nor whichever John
you choose to treat of, nor even Mary herself

is seated in any heaven separate
from these spirits that have appeared to you,
nor has their existence more or fewer years;

but all make up the beauty of the First
Circle, and know its sweet life differently
as more, or less, they feel the eternal breath.

That you perceive them here is not because
this is their allotted sphere, but is a marker
of the rank in heaven that is least exalted.

To speak like this is suited to your nature,
for only by sensation can it grasp
what it must then make fit for the intellect;

which too is why the Scriptures condescend
to your capacity, and give God feet
and hands while meaning something different,

and why the Church has shown with human faces
Michael and Gabriel, and that other angel
who helped Tobias cure his father's blindness.

The way Timaeus reasons of the soul
is not like what is here revealed, for he
seems to take what he tells us literally.

He says the soul returns to its own star
from which he thinks it had been plucked away
when nature lent it to inform a body;

though maybe his opinion should be taken
not quite as his words sound, but differently,
and then his meaning need not be derided:

for if he means that to these spheres returns
the credit for their influence, or the blame,
perhaps his arrow has struck something true.

This was the principle, misunderstood,
that misled almost all the world once, causing
stars to be named for Jove, or Mars, or Mercury.

The other hesitation that disturbs you
is not so dangerous, for its toxins could not
cause you to stray from me entirely.

That heavenly justice can appear unjust
to human eyes is proof of faith and not
a starting-point for wicked heresy.

But since your ingenuity's well equipped
to grasp and understand this truth, I will,
as you would wish, explain and satisfy you.

If violence is when the one who suffers
colludes in nothing with the violator,
then not for that have these souls been excused:

for a will that cannot will is not extinguished,
but does as nature does in fire, though force
blast it aside again a thousand times.

So if the will bows greatly, or even a little,
it connives with the coercer; and that these did,
who might still have fled back to holy ground.

If their will had remained whole and unbroken
like that which held St Lawrence to the grid-iron
or made Mucius harsh to his own hand,

it would have driven them back onto the pathway
they'd been dragged from, as soon as they were free;
but such heroic will is rare indeed.

And by these words, if you have harvested
their meaning rightly, now the doubt is quashed
that would have otherwise gone on bothering you.

But now before your gaze another track
runs cross-wise, such that, by your own devices
you'd not get past it till you were exhausted.

I have put this in your mind as certainty:
no soul in bliss can ever tell a lie
because it dwells so near the primal Truth;

and yet you've just heard from Piccarda that
Costanza never lost her love of the veil,
so here perhaps it seems she contradicts me.

It has often happened, brother, that, to escape
danger, against a person's deepest wishes
things have been done that should not have been done;

thus, at his father's plea, Alcmeon murdered
his own mother, and thereby made himself
pitiless, in meeting the demands of piety.

At this point I want you to recognize
will with duress can be so mixed it cannot
but act in ways that are inexcusable.

The absolute will does not consent to the crime,
but has consented insofar as it fears
that shrinking back will plunge it in worse trouble.

So when Piccarda says that, what she means
is the absolute will, and I the other, so
we both speak truth and there's no contradiction.'

Such was the rippling of the holy river
that flowed forth from the fount of all truth-telling;
it brought peace to my contradictory urgings.

'O you, beloved of the first Lover, O divine one',
I said then, 'you whose speech so floods and warms me
that more and more it draws me into life,

all my affection has not depth enough
to answer and reward you, grace for grace;
may He that sees, and can, may He do so!

I clearly see that nothing satisfies
our intellect until it's lighted by
that truth beyond whose bound no truth extends.

There it can settle like a beast in its den
once it has joined with that; and it can join
with that or all our longings would be futile.

Born from these longings, at the foot of truth
doubt springs like a shoot, and it is nature that
compels us on from peak to peak to the summit.

By this emboldened, by this given security,
with reverence, Lady, I enquire of you
about another question that disturbs me.

I want to know if a man can make amends
to you for broken vows with other goods
that will not always on your scales weigh light?'

Then Beatrice looked at me with eyes so full
of sparks of love, and so divine, that all
my strength was overcome, and turned its back,

and I stood almost lost, with eyes downcast.

p. 18 'An African Exile in Australia':
as a young child I lived in South Africa. Visiting Australia brought back echoes of that country; this poem attempts to convey something of the quality of that experience.

p. 20 'Yamane-san':
a woman I knew when I lived in Japan in the 1960s told me this memory from her childhood.

p.22 'Untarryingly-coming':
I have taken the liberty of inserting a hyphen into this adjective, which is borrowed from Michael Hamburger's translation of Celan's 'Todtnauberg', in which Celan describes visiting Heidegger.

p. 26 'Ages of Man: Breaking the News':
this poem was inspired in part by an exhibition at the British Museum of objects and figurines from the last Ice Age. It attempts impressionistically to describe some of the changes in relations between the sexes from the Ice Age to the present.

p. 28 'The Uses of Mythology':
the Poussin epigraph is from a letter he wrote to a patron who had asked him to paint another biblical scene.

p. 34 'In St Peter's, Rome':
the Kali Yuga is the Hindu equivalent of the classical 'Age of Lead', the fourth phase of human history, when society is breaking down. It's said that in the Kali Yuga the heroic austerities of the past are no longer possible, but one can still tell the truth.

p. 37 'Saint Augustine's Eulogy for his Mother, Saint Monica':
when Augustine was 33, urged by Monica he became
a Christian; he abandoned his mistress and his career
as a professor of rhetoric, and returned from Milan to
Carthage with Monica and his son Adeodatus. The party
were delayed in Ostia, and while they were there Monica
died. In this poem, I imagine Augustine's state of mind at
the time of her funeral, when his promising and brilliant
future had suddenly vanished, and it was quite unclear
what he would do.

p. 40 'George Fox in Lichfield':
George Fox, founder of the Quakers, describes this incident
in his Journal.

p. 42 'The Buddha Amitābha':
he refused in his previous incarnation to become a Buddha
unless he could be true to forty-eight Vows, of which the
18th is the most famous. This poem attempts to summarise
it.

p.44 'M. Lévinas Advises the Prince':
this passage is adapted from Emmanuel Lévinas' paper,
'Ethics as First Philosophy'

p. 53 Der Kürenberger:
one of the earliest of the *Minnesinger*, the Germanic
precursors of the troubadours. A wandering poet in the
Danube region, he wrote in the twelfth century.

p. 57 Dante: 'Amore e'l cor gentil':
this sonnet is from *La Vita Nuova*. In Dante, as in Chaucer,
the word *gentle* still carries the implication of *noble*.

p. 63 'Poem for Translation into the Thirteenth Century':
'irons' and 'Sirens' rhyme nicely in Scotland, though
perhaps not elsewhere in the English-speaking world.

'Purgatorio XVII':
p. 68 "The wickedness of her..."
Dante emerges from the dark cloud when he recognises
the hugely destructive effects of 'wrath' by recalling
three stories. They are: 1. the myth of Procne and
Philomela (Ovid: Metamorphoses); 2. the biblical story
of Haman's hatred of the Jews (the "one crucified" here
is Haman) (Book of Esther); 3. the story of Aeneas'
arrival in Latium: Lavinia's mother Amata killed herself
because she believed, mistakenly, that Lavinia's lover
Turnus had been killed by Aeneas who would now
marry Lavinia (Virgil: *Aeneid*).'
p. 70 "... like a wing brushing my face":
At the threshold of Purgatory, an angel wrote seven Ps
on Dante's brow (for *peccata*, sins). As he leaves each
terrace, one P is brushed away.
p. 72 "...must then stamp his evil on the other.":
These three tercets have described the sins repented for
in the three Circles Dante has already passed through:
pride, envy, and wrath.
p. 72 "This other good...":
These things that are good in themselves but lose their
goodness when they are loved without what keeps
them in proportion, namely, the love of 'essential
Goodness'.

'Paradiso Canto IV':
p. 73 "... that had made the King become unjustly cruel":
Daniel not only interpreted Nebuchadnezzar's dream,
he first told the King what the King had dreamt.

Similarly, Beatrice not only answers Dante's questions, but she first tells him what questions he is troubled by.

p. 74 "… they feel the eternal breath":
Dante is saying that souls in Paradise do have different experiences, not because they are assigned to different places, but in accordance with their differing capacities to experience God's presence in the 'First Circle', the Empyrean. (The word translated here as 'breath' could equally be translated as 'spirit').

p. 75 "perhaps his arrow has struck something true.":
Though souls do not return to the stars, Dante believes that 'the stars' influence human motives.

p. 78 "'… we both speak truth and there's no contradiction.'":
Aquinas distinguished between the 'absolute' and the 'conditioned' will, so when Beatrice says 'the other', she means the conditioned.

BIOGRAPHICAL NOTE

DAVID MACLEOD BLACK was born in South Africa, brought up in Scotland. He has published six collections of poetry and also a volume of translations of Goethe. A selection of his early work appeared in the Penguin Modern Poets series in 1968. In the 1990s he translated a number of Goethe's poems, including the 'Roman Elegies', and together with Robert Chandler, Elizabeth Cook, Martha Kapos, Robin Leanse and Carole Satyamurti, he was one of a group of poets who met each month to discuss each other's work. The composition of this group has varied over the years: Satyamurti and Leanse left, Christopher Reid was a member for a time, but the group still continues and Black has described it as invaluable.

From 1998 to 2008 he was a frequent book-reviewer for *Poetry London*. *Love as Landscape Painter*, his translations of Goethe, appeared in 2007; *Claiming Kindred*, appeared in 2011.

He has also published papers on literary and psychoanalytic themes. In 2006 he edited *Psychoanalysis and Religion in the 21st Century: Competitors or Collaborators?* (New Library of Psychoanalysis), and in 2011 he published a collection of essays on values, under the title *Why Things Matter: the place of values in science, psychoanalysis and religion* (Routledge).

www.dmblack.net

Titles in Arc Publications'
POETRY FROM THE UK / IRELAND include:

D. M. BLACK
Claiming Kindred

JAMES BYRNE
Blood / Sugar
White Coins

TONY CURTIS
What Darkness Covers
The Well in the Rain
folk
Approximately in the Key of C

JULIA DARLING
Indelible, Miraculous
COLLECTED POEMS

LINDA FRANCE
You are Her
Reading the Flowers

KATHERINE GALLAGHER
Circus-Apprentice
Carnival Edge
Acres of Light

RICHARD GWYN
Sad Giraffe Café

GLYN HUGHES
A Year in the Bull-Box

MICHAEL HASLAM
The Music Laid Her Songs in Language
A Sinner Saved by Grace
A Cure for Woodness

MICHAEL HULSE
The Secret History
Half-Life

CHRISTOPHER JAMES
Farewell to the Earth

BRIAN JOHNSTONE
The Book of Belongings
Dry Stone Work

JOEL LANE
Trouble in the Heartland
The Autumn Myth

SOPHIE MAYER
(O)

PETE MORGAN
August Light

MICHAEL O'NEILL
Wheel
Gangs of Shadow

MARY O'DONNELL
The Ark Builders
Those April Fevers

IAN POPLE
An Occasional Lean-to
Saving Spaces

PAUL STUBBS
The Icon Maker
The End of the Trial of Man

GEROGE SZIRTES & CAROL WATTS
Fifty-six

LORNA THORPE
A Ghost in My House
Sweet Torture of Breathing

ROISIN TIERNEY
The Spanish-Italian Border

MICHELENE WANDOR
Musica Transalpina
Music of the Prophets
Natural Chemistry

JACKIE WILLS
Fever Tree
Commandments
Woman's Head as Jug

www.ingramcontent.com/pod-product-compliance
Lightning Source LLC
Chambersburg PA
CBHW021339060726
47591CB00006B/2099